STORIES OF THE EAST

LEONARD WOOLF

This edition copyright © The Long Riders' Guild Press

All rights reserved. Without limiting the rights under copyright reserved above, no part of this publication may be reproduced, stored in or introduced into a retrieval system, or transmitted, in any form or by any means (electronic, mechanical, photocopying, recording or otherwise) without the prior written permission of The Long Riders' Guild Press.

The Long Riders' Guild Press

www.classictravelbooks.com
www.horsetravelbooks.com

ISBN: 1-59048-062-7

First printed and published by Leonard and Virginia Woolf at the Hogarth Press, Hogarth House, Richmond. 1921

Introduction

Christopher Ondaatje

Leonard Woolf is perhaps best remembered in Sri Lanka for his novel *The Village in the Jungle* (1913), rather than for his professed anti-imperialism developed during his short seven year stint (1904-1911) as a member of the Ceylon civil service – a small group of white administrators who ruled the colony. However, the three short stories "A Tale Told by Moonlight", "The Two Brahmans" and "Pearls and Swine" published under the umbrella title *Stories of the East* are less well known. Woolf wrote them some time after his return from Ceylon in 1911 but they were not published by the Hogarth Press until 1921. They were then republished in 1962 as an appendix to Woolf's *Diaries in Ceylon* where their title was changed, for some unknown reason, to the slightly different *Stories from the East*. Although they sold poorly at the time, and have been largely overlooked by literary critics since, all three stories are of interest – especially in understanding their author's mind. As Mervyn de Silva notes in his introduction to *Diaries in Ceylon*, the stories are clearly the work of "an intelligence of fine quality, morally aware, humane and inquisitive but, most of all, disturbed by the impact of the East, and uneasy before its strange, exacting demands on understanding."

Woolf has been criticised for his first story "A Tale Told by Moonlight" as being a ploy to avoid blame for the story's content – an affair between an expatriate

Englishman and a prostitute. This was a device he used in his other racist stories on Ceylon. However, Anindyo Roy, the author of *Civility and Empire: Literature and Culture in British India, 1822 – 1922,* views the story much more perceptively in being a "real" dramatisation of a trauma that had its source in Woolf's personal experiences in Ceylon and that exposed to him the chasm between the fantasy and the reality of imperialism. The possibility of knowing the "real" is betrayed in the tale when the story-teller shows "the power of the white man to insert the woman into a system of colonial exchange as a way to hold on to its own fantasy."

The clash between caste values and the individual's values is at the heart of Woolf's second short story "The Two Brahmans", which is set in Jaffna, though the town is given its Tamil name Yalpanam. Woolf explains that a member of one caste cannot eat with or marry into another caste, or work at the work of another caste, for their own caste will then be defiled and they will lose their status. But the Brahmins of the story are not content with the time-honoured caste traditions. One persuades a reluctant fisherman to teach him to fish; and the other pollutes his caste by carrying earth on his head. Both Brahmins are "cast out" from the Brahmin caste by the other Brahmins. Years pass and the transgressions are forgotten only to flare up again when a young man and woman, descendants of the two families, fall in love and want to marry. When Woolf wrote the story Christian missions (especially in the Jaffna area) and the introduction of English education by the Government were already ending Ceylonese caste barriers.

Pessimism is the dominant note of Woolf's finest short story "Pearls and Swine" about a pearl fishery.

Introduction

There is little sign in it of the exotic elements found in his two other stories. Besides capturing the strangeness of the pearl fishery and the gritty texture of colonial life, "Pearls and Swine", with its perfectly judged title, is a literary achievement that is almost, though not quite, on a par with the classic Kipling stories of India that Woolf admired. As in "A Tale Told by Moonlight" the eastern setting is distanced by the story's starting in England where five Englishmen, one an Anglo-Indian District Commissioner, find themselves together by chance in the smoking room of a seaside hotel in Torquay late in the evening when the conversation turns to the subject of the East. The Commissioner launches into his story of the East – a description of a pearl fishery somewhere on the south coast of India which closely resembles the one Woolf had known in Ceylon – with sharp-edged comments on the Government. The tragic story involves a sordid tale of exploitation of both whites and natives all over the Colonial East, and brings different political perspectives on imperialism into discussion.

There is one other important coda to my introduction for *Stories of the East*, and curiously it is recounted by Woolf in the fourth volume of his autobiography, *Downhill All the Way*. In 1921 Hamilton Fyfe declared in the *Daily Mail* that "Pearls and Swine" deserved to be ranked with the great stories of the world. This was picked up by the American literary agent Henry Holt, who wrote to Woolf offering to place the story in America for him. Woolf sent Holt a copy of the book but "when he read the story, it was obviously a bit of a shock to him, being a good deal too plain spoken for the two hundred pound bracket in the United States of America. He wanted to tone it down a bit – he called this euphemistically a 'few artistic alterations'". Woolf refused, saying he could not bear to rewrite anything from long ago and suggested Holt deal with the matter himself. Holt sought the opinion of another American literary agent, Ann Watkins, and she, said Woolf, "also thought the story a masterpiece but was also horrified by it and the idea of offering it to the American market." Watkins reckoned that perhaps only two magazines would touch the story: "You see, we here in the States are still provincial enough to want the sugar-coated pill, we don't like facts, we don't like to have to face them." This was quite astute – and echoed Woolf's own ambivalence in trying to present the "real" in his stories.

Yet Holt pursued him relentlessly, writing letters that promised commercial success if Woolf would only tailor his style to the American market. But Woolf had too much integrity to alter his stories for money. It was a brave decision then, and a wonderful thing now that at long last Classic Travel Books has taken the plunge, published *Stories of the East* on both sides of the Atlantic, and rectified an eighty-six year old mistake.

Sir Christopher Ondaatje is the author of *Woolf in Ceylon*.

CONTENTS

A Tale Told by Moonlight 7
The Two Brahmans 23
Pearls and Swine 35

www.classictravelbooks.com

A Tale Told By Moonlight

Many people did not like Jessop. He had rather a brutal manner sometimes of telling brutal things – the truth, he called it. "They don't like it", he once said to me in a rare moment of confidence. "But why the devil shouldn't they? They pretend these sorts of things, battle, murder, and sudden death, are so real – more real than white kid gloves and omnibuses and rose leaves – and yet when you give them the real thing, they curl up like school girls. It does them good, you know, does them a world of good".

They didn't like it and they didn't altogether like him. He was a sturdy thick set man, very strong, a dark reserved man with black eyebrows which met over his nose. He had knocked about the world a good deal. He appealed to me in many ways; I liked to meet him. He had fished things up out of life, curious grim things, things which may have disgusted but which certainly fascinated as well.

The last time I saw him we were both staying with Alderton, the novelist. Mrs. Alderton was away – recruiting after annual childbirth, I think. The other guests were Pemberton, who was recruiting after his annual book of verses, and Smith, Hanson Smith, the critic.

It was a piping hot June day, and we strolled out after dinner in the cool moonlight down the great fields which lead to the river. It was very cool, very beautiful, very romantic lying there on the grass above the river bank, watching the great trees in the moonlight and the silver water slipping along so musically to the sea. We grew silent and sentimental – at least I know I did.

Two figures came slowly along the bank, a young man with his arm round a girl's waist. They passed just under where we were lying without seeing us. We heard the murmur of his words and in the shadow of the trees they stopped and we heard the sound of their kisses.

I heard Pemberton mutter:

A boy and girl if the good fates please
    Making love say,
The happier they.
Come up out of the light of the moon
And let them pass as they will, too soon
With the bean flowers boon
And the blackbird's tune
And May and June.

It loosed our tongues and we began to speak – all of us except Jessop – as men seldom speak together, of love. We were sentimental, romantic. We told stories of our first loves. We looked back with regret, with yearning to our youth and to love. We were passionate in our belief in it, love, the great passion, the real thing which had just passed us by so closely in the moonlight.

We talked like that for an hour or so, I suppose, and Jessop never opened his lips. Whenever I looked at him, he was watching the river gliding by and he was frowning. At last there was a pause; we were all silent for a minute or two and then Jessop began to speak

"You talk as if you believed all that: it's queer, damned queer. A boy kissing a girl in the moonlight and you call it love and poetry and romance. But you know as well as I do it isn't. It's just a flicker of the body it will be cold, dead this time next year."

He had stopped but nobody spoke and then he continued slowly, almost sadly. "We're old men and middle-aged men, aren't we? We've all done that. We remember how we kissed like that in the moonlight or no light at all. It was pleasant; Lord. I'm not denying that – but some of us are married and some of us aren't. We're middle-aged – well, think of your wives, think of – " he stopped again. I looked round. The others were moving uneasily. It was this kind of thing that people didn't like in Jessop. He spoke again.

"It's you novelists who're responsible, you know. You've made a world in which everyone is always falling in love – but its not this world. Here it's the flicker of the body

I don't say there isn't such a thing. There is. I've seen it, but it's rare, as rare as – as – a perfect horse, an Arab once said to me. The real thing, it's too queer to be anything but the rarest; it's the queerest thing in the world. Think of it for a moment, chucking out of your mind all this business of kisses and moonlight and marriages. A miserable tailless ape buzzed round through space on this half cold cinder of an earth, a timid bewildered ignorant savage little beast always fighting for bare existence. And suddenly it runs up against another miserable naked tailless ape and immediately everything that it has ever known dies out of its little puddle of a mind, itself, its beastly body, its puny wandering desires. the wretched fight for existence, the whole world. And instead there comes a flame of passion for something in that other naked ape, not for her body or her mind or her soul, but for something beautiful mysterious everlasting – yes that's it, the everlasting passion in her which has flamed up in him. He goes buzzing on through space, but he isn't tired or bewildered or ignorant any more; he can see his way now even among the stars.

And that's love, the love which you novelists scatter about so freely. What does it mean? I don't understand it; it's queer beyond anything I've ever struck. It isn't animal – that's the point – or vegetable or mineral. Not one man in ten thousand feels it and not one woman in twenty thousand. How can they? It's feeling, a passion immense, steady, enduring. But not one person in twenty thousand ever feels anything at all for more than a second, and then it's only a feeble ripple on the smooth surface of their unconsciousness.

O yes, we've all been in love. We can all remember the kisses we gave and the kisses given to us in the moonlight. But that's the body. The body's damnably exacting. It wants to kiss and to be kissed at certain times and seasons. It isn't particular however; give it moonlight and young lips and it's soon satisfied. It's only when we don't pay for it that we call it romance and love, and the most we would ever pay is a £5 note.

But it's not love, not the other, the real, the mysterious thing.

That too exists, I've seen it, I tell you, but it's rare. Lord, it's rare. I'm middle aged. I've seen men, thousands of them, all over the world, known them, too, made it my business to know them, it interests me, a hobby like collecting stamps. And I've only known two cases of real love.

And neither of them had anything to do with kisses and moonlight. Why should they? When it comes, it comes in strange ways and places, like most real things perversely and unreasonably. I suppose scientifically it's all right – it's what the mathematician calls the law of chances.

I'll tell you about one of them.

There was a man – you may have read his books, so I won't give you his name – though he's dead now – I'll call him Reynolds. He was at Rugby with me and also at Corpus. He was a thin feeble-looking chap, very nervous, with pale face and long pale hands. He was bullied a good deal at school; he was what they call a smug. I knew him rather well; there seemed to me to be something in him somewhere, some power of feeling under the nervousness and shyness. I can't say it ever came out, but he interested me.

I went East and he stayed at home and wrote novels. I read them; very romantic they were too, the usual ideas of men and women and love. But they were clever in many ways, especially psychologically, as it was called. He was a success, he made money.

I used to get letters from him about once in three months, so when he came travelling to the east it was arranged that he would stay a week with me. I was in Colombo at that time right in the passenger route. I found him one day on the deck of a P and O just the same as I had last seen him in Oxford, except for the large sun helmet on his head and the blue glasses on his nose. And when I got him back to the bungalow and began to talk with him on the broad verandah, I found that he was still just the same inside too. The years had not touched him anywhere, he had not in the ordinary sense lived at all. He had stood aside – do you see what I mean? – from shyness, nervousness, the remembrance and fear of being bullied, and watched other people living. He knew a good deal about how other people. think, the little tricks and mannerisms of life and novels, but he didn't know how they felt. I expect he had never felt anything himself, except fear and shyness: he hadn't really ever known a man, and he had certainly never known a woman.

Well he wanted to see life, to understand it, to feel it. He had travelled 7000 miles to do so. He was very keen to begin, he wanted to see life all round, up and down, inside and out; he told me so as we looked out on the palm trees and the glimpse of the red road beyond and the unending stream of brown men and women upon it.

I began to show him life in the East. I took him to the clubs, the club where they play tennis and gossip, the club where they play bridge and gossip, the club where they just sit in the long chairs and gossip. I introduced him to scores of men who

A Tale Told By Moonlight

asked him to have a drink and to scores of women who asked him whether he liked Colombo. He didn't get on with them at all, he said 'No thank you' to the men and 'Yes, very much' to the women. He was shy and felt uncomfortable, out of his element with these fat flannelled merchants, fussy civil servants, and their whining wives ,and daughters.

In the evening we sat on my verandah and talked. We talked about life and his novels and romance and love even. I liked him, you know; he interested me, there was something in him which had never come out. But he had got hold of life at the wrong end somehow, he couldn't deal with it or the people in it at all. He had the novelist's view of life and – with all respect to you, Alderton – it doesn't work.

I suppose the devil came into me that evening. Reynolds had talked so much about seeing life that at last I thought: "By love, I'll show him a side of life *he's* never seen before at any rate". I called the servant and told him to fetch two rickshaws.

We bowled along the dusty roads past the lake and into the native quarter. All the smells of the East rose up and hung heavy upon the damp hot air in the narrow streets. I watched Reynolds' face in the moonlight, the scared look which always showed upon it; I very nearly repented and turned back. Even now I'm not sure whether I'm sorry that I didn't. At any rate I didn't, and at last we drew up in front of a low mean looking house standing back a little from the road.

There was one of those queer native wooden

doors made in two halves; the top half was open and through it one saw an empty white-washed room lighted by a lamp fixed in the wall. We went in and I shut the door top and bottom behind us. At the other end were two steps leading up to another room. Suddenly there came the sound of bare feet running and giggles of laughter, and ten or twelve girls, some naked and some half clothed in bright red or bright orange clothes, rushed down the steps upon us. We were surrounded, embraced, caught up in their arms and carried into the next room. We lay upon sofas with them. There was nothing but sofas and an old piano in the room.

They knew me well in the place, – you can imagine what it was – I often went there. Apart from anything else, it interested me. The girls were all Tamils and Sinhalese. It always reminded me somehow of the Arabian Nights; that room when you came into it so bare and empty, and then the sudden rush of laughter, the pale yellow naked women, the brilliant colours of the cloths, the white teeth, all appearing so suddenly in the doorway up there at the end of the room. And the girls themselves interested me; I used to sit and talk to them for hours in their own language; they didn't as a rule understand English. They used to tell me all about themselves, queer pathetic stories often. They came from villages almost always, little native villages hidden far away among rice fields and coconut trees, and they had drifted somehow into this hovel in the warren of filth and smells which we and our civilization had attracted about us.

Poor Reynolds, he was very uncomfortable at

A Tale Told By Moonlight

first. He didn't how what to do in the least or where to look. He stammered out yes and no to the broken English sentences which the girls repeated like parrots to him. They soon got tired of kissing him and came over to me to tell me their little troubles and ask me for advice –; all of them that is, except one.

She was called Celestinahami and was astonishingly beautiful. Her skin was the palest of pale gold with a glow in it, very rare in the fair native women. The delicate innocent beauty of a child was in her face; and her eyes, Lord, her eyes immense, deep, dark and melancholy which looked as if they knew and understood and felt everything in the world. She never wore anything coloured, just a white cloth wrapped round her waist with one end thrown over the left shoulder. She carried about her an air of slowness and depth and mystery of silence and of innocence.

She lay full length on the sofa with her chin on her hands, looking up into Reynolds' face and smiling at him. The white cloth had slipped down and her breasts were bare. She was a Sinhalese, a cultivator's daughter, from a little village up in the hills: her place was in the green rice fields weeding, or in the little compound under the palm trees pounding rice, but she lay on the dirty sofa and asked Reynolds in her soft broken English whether he would have a drink.

It began in him with pity. 'I saw the pity of it, Jessop', he said to me afterwards, 'the pity of it'. He lost his shyness, he began to talk to her in his gentle cultivated voice; she didn't understand a word, but she looked up at him with her great innocent eyes and smiled at him. He even stroked her hand and her arm. She smiled at him still, and said her few soft clipped English sentences. He looked into her eyes that understood nothing but seemed to understand everything, and then it came out at last; the power to feel, the power that so few have, the flame. the passion; love, the real thing.

It was the real thing, I tell you; I ought to know; he stayed on in my bungalow day after day, and night after night he went down to that hovel among the filth and smells. It wasn't the body, it wasn't kisses and moonlight. He wanted her of course, he wanted her body and soul; but he wanted something else: the same passion, the same fine strong thing that he felt moving in himself. She was everything to him that was beautiful and great and pure, she was what she looked, what he read in the depths of her eyes. And she might have been – why not? She might have been all that and more – there's no reason why such a thing shouldn't happen, shouldn't have happened even. One can believe that still. But the chances .are all against it. She was a prostitute in a Colombo brothel, a simple soft little golden-skinned animal with nothing in the depths of the eyes at all. It was the law of chances at work as usual, you know.

It was tragic and it was at the same time wonderfully ridiculous. At times he saw things as they were, the bare truth, the hopelessness of it, And then he was so ignorant of life, fumbling about so curiously with all the little things in it. It was too much for him; he tried to shoot himself with a

A Tale Told By Moonlight

revolver which he had bought at the Army and Navy Stores before he sailed; but he couldn't because he had forgotten how to put in the cartridges.

Yes, I burst in on him sitting at a table in his room fumbling with the thing. It was one of those rotten old-fashioned things with a piece of steel that snaps down over the chamber to prevent the cartridges falling out. He hadn't discovered how to snap it back in order to get the cartridges in. The man who sold him that revolver, instead of an automatic pistol, as he ought to have done, saved his life.

And then I talked to him seriously. I quoted his own novel to him. It was absurdly romantic, unreal, his novel, but it preached as so many of them do, that you should face facts first and then live your life out to the uttermost. I quoted it to him. Then I told him baldly brutally what the girl was – not a bit what he thought her, what his passion went out to – a nice simple soft little animal like the bitch at my feet that starved herself if I left her for a day. ·'It's the truth', I said to him, 'as true as that you're really in love, in love with something that doesn't exist behind those great eyes. It's dangerous, damned dangerous because it's real – and that's why it's rare. But it's no good shooting yourself with that thing. You've got to get on board the next P & O, that's what you've got to do. And if you won't do that, why practise what you preach and live your life out, and take the risks."

He asked me what I meant.

'The risks?' I said. 'I can see what they are, and

if you'd take them, you're taking the worst odds ever offered a man. But there they are. Take the girl and see what you can make of life with her. You can buy her out of that place for fifteen rupees'.

I was wrong, I suppose. I ought to have put him in irons and shipped him off next day. But I don't know, really I don't know.

He took the risks any way. We bought her out, it cost twenty rupees. I got them a little house down the coast on the seashore, a little house surrounded by palm trees. The sea droned away sleepily right under the verandah. It was to be an idyll of the East; he was to live there for ever with her and write novels on the verandah.

And, by God, he was happy – at first. I used to go down there and stay with them pretty often. He taught her English and she taught him Sinhalese. He started to write a novel about the East: it would have been a good novel I think, full of strength and happiness and sun and reality – if it had been finished. But it never was. He began to see the truth, the damned hard unpleasant truths that I had told him that night in the Colombo bungalow. And the cruelty of it was that he still had that rare power to feel, that he still felt. It was the real thing. you see, and the real thing is – didn't I say – immense, steady, enduring. It is; I believe that still. He was in love, but he knew now what she was like. He couldn't speak to her and she couldn't speak to him, she couldn't understand him. He was a civilized cultivated intelligent nervous little man and she – she was an animal, dumb and stupid and beautiful.

I watched it happening, I had foretold it. but I cursed myself for not having stopped it, scores of times. He loved her but she tortured him. People would say, I suppose, that she got on his nerves. It's a good enough description. But the cruellest thing of all was that she had grown to love him, love him like an animal, as a bitch loves her master". Jessop stopped. We waited for him to go on but he didn't. The leaves rustled gently in the breeze; the river murmured softly below us; up in the woods 1 heard a nightingale singing. "Well, and then?" Alderton asked at last in a rather peevish voice.

"And then? Damn that nightingale!" said Jessop. "I wish I hadn't begun this story. It happened so long ago: I thought I had forgotten to feel it, to feel that I was responsible for what happened then. There's another sort of love; it isn't the body and it isn't the flame, it's the love of dogs and women, at any rate of those slow, big-eyed women of the East. It's the love of a slave, the patient, consuming love for a master, for his kicks and his caresses, for his kisses and his blows. That was the sort of love which grew up slowly in Celestinahami for Reynolds. But it wasn't what he wanted, it was that, I expect, more than anything which got on his nerves.

She used to follow him about the bungalow like a dog. He wanted to talk to her about his novel and she only understood how to pound and cook rice. It exasperated him, made him unkind, cruel. And when he looked into her patient mysterious eyes he saw behind them what he had fallen in love with, what be knew didn't exist. It began to drive him mad.

And she – she of course couldn't even understand what was the matter. She saw that he was unhappy, she thought she had done something wrong. She reasoned like a child that it was because she wasn't like the white ladies whom she used to see in Colombo. So she went and bought stays and white cotton stockings and shoes, and she squeezed herself into them. But the stays and the shoes and stockings didn't do her any good. It couldn't go on like that. At last I induced Reynolds to go away. He was to continue his travels but he was coming back – he said so over and over again to me and to Celestinahami. Meanwhile she was well provided for; a deed was executed: the house and the coconut trees and the little compound by the sea were to be hers – a generous settlement, a donatio inter vivos, as the lawyers call it – void, eh? – or voidable? – because for an immoral consideration. Lord! I'm nearly forgetting my law, but I believe the law holds that only future consideration of that sort can be immoral. How wise, how just, isn't it? The past cannot be immoral; it's done with, wiped out – but the future? Yes, it's only the future that counts.

So Reynolds wiped out his past and Celestinahami by the help of a dirty Burgher lawyer and a deed of gift and a ticket issued by Thomas Cook and Son for a berth in a P & O bound for Aden. I went on board to see him off and I shook his hand and told him encouragingly that everything would be all right. I never saw Reynolds again but I saw Celestinahami once.

It was at the inquest two days after the Moldavia

sailed for Aden. She was lying on a dirty wooden board on trestles in the dingy mud-plastered room behind the court. Yes, I identified her:

Celestinahami – I never knew her other name. She lay there in her stays and pink skirt and white stockings and white shoes. They had found her floating in the sea that lapped the foot of the convent garden below the little bungalow – bobbing up and down in her stays and pink skirt and white stockings and shoes".

* * * * * * *

Jessop stopped. No one spoke for a minute or two. Then Hanson Smith stretched himself, yawned, and got up.

"Battle, murder, and sentimentality", he said. "You're as bad as the rest of them, Jessop. I'd like to hear your other case – but it's too late, I'm off to bed".

The Two Brahmans

Yalpanam is a very large town in the north of Ceylon; but nobody who suddenly found himself in it would believe this. Only in two or three streets is there any bustle or stir of people. It is like a gigantic village that for centuries has slept and grown, and sleeps and grows, under a forest of coconut trees and fierce sun. And the streets are the same, dazzling dusty roads between high fences made of the dried leaves of the coconut palms. Behind the fences, and completely hidden by them, are the compounds; and in the compounds still more hidden under the palms and orange and lime trees are the huts and houses of the Tamils who live there.

The north of the town lies, as it has lain for centuries, sleeping by the side of the blue lagoon, and there is a hut standing now in a compound by the side of the lagoon, where it had stood for centuries. In this hut there lived a man called Chellaya who was by caste a Brahman, and in the compound next to Chellaya's lived another Brahman called Chittampalam, and in all the other fifty or sixty compounds around them lived other Brahmans. They belonged to the highest of an castes in Yalpanam, and they could not eat food with or touch or marry into any other caste, nor could they carry earth on their heads or work at any trade, without being defiled or losing caste. Therefore all the Brahmans live together in this quarter of the town, so that they may not be defiled but may marry off their sons and daughters to daughters and sons of other Brahmans. Chellaya and Chittampalam and all the Brahmans knew that they and their fathers and their fathers' fathers had lived in the same way by the side of the blue lagoon under the palm trees for many thousands of years. They did no work, for there was no need to work. The dhobi or washer caste man, who washed the clothes of Brahmans and of no other caste, washed their white cloths and in return was given rice and allowed to be present at weddings and funerals. And there was the barber caste man who shaved the Brahmans and no other caste. And half a mile from their compounds were their Brahman rice fields in which Chellaya and each of the other Brahmans had shares; some shares had descended to them from their fathers and their grandfathers and great-grandfathers and so on from the first Brahmans, and other shares had been brought to them as dowry with their wives. These fields were sown twice a year, and the work of cultivation was done by Mukkuwa caste men. This is a custom, that Mukkuwa caste men cultivate the rice fields of Brahmans, and it had been a custom for many thousands of years.

Chellaya was forty-five and Chittampalam was forty-two, and they had lived, as all Brahmans lived, in the houses in which they had been born. There can be no doubt that quite suddenly one of the gods, or rather devils, laid a spell upon these two compounds. And this is how it happened.

Chellaya had married, when he was 14, a plump Brahman girl of 12 who had borne him three sons and two daughters. He had married off both his daughters without giving very large dowries and his sons had all married girls who had brought them large dowries. No man ought to have been happier, though his wife was too talkative and had a sharp tongue. And for 45 years Chellaya lived happily the life which all good Brahmans should live. Every morning he ate his rice cakes and took his bath at the well in his compound and went to the temple of Siva. There he talked until midday to his wife's brother and his daughter's husband's father about Nallatampi, their neighbour, who was on bad terms with them, about the price of rice, and about a piece of land which he had been thinking of buying for the last five years. After the midday meal of rice and curry, cooked by his wife, he dozed through the afternoon; and then, when the sun began to lose its power, he went down to the shore of the blue lagoon and sat there until nightfall.

This was Chellaya's passion, to sit by the side of the still, shining, blue waters and look over them at the far-off islands, which flickered and quivered in the mirage of heat. The wind, dying down at evening, just murmured in the palms behind him. The heat lay like something tangible and soothing upon the earth. And Chellaya waited eagerly for the hour when the fishermen come out with their cast-nets and wade out into the shallow water after the fish. How eagerly he waited all day for that moment; even in the temple when talking about Nallatampi, whom he hated, the vision of those unruffled waters would continually rise up before him, and of the lean men lifting their feet so gently first one and then the other, in order not to make a splash or a ripple, and bending forward with the nets in their hands ready to cast. And then the joy of the capture, the great leaping twisting silver fish in the net at last. He began to hate his compound and his fat wife and the interminable talk in the temple, and those long dreary evenings when he stood under his umbrella at the side of his rice field and watched the Mukkuwas ploughing or sowing or reaping.

As Chellaya grew older he became more and more convinced that the only pleasure in life was to be a fisher and to catch fish. This troubled him not a little, for the Fisher caste is a low caste and no Brahman had ever caught a fish. It would be utter pollution and losing of caste to him. One day however when he went down to sit in his accustomed place by the side of the lagoon, he found a fisherman sitting on the sand there mending his net.

"Fisher", said Chellaya, "could one who has never had a net in his hand and was no longer young learn how to cast it?"

Chellaya was a small round fat man, but he had spoken with great dignity. The fisher knew at once that he was a Brahman and salaamed, touching the ground with his forehead.

"Lord", he said, "the boy learns to cast the net when he is still at his mother's breast".

"O foolish dog of a fisher", said Chellaya pretending to be very angry, "can you not understand? Suppose one who was not a fisher and was well on in years wished to fish – for a vow or even for play – could such a one learn to cast the net?"

The old fisherman screwed up his wrinkled face and looked up at Chellaya doubtfully.

"Lord", he said, "I cannot tell. For how could such a thing be? To the fisher his net, as the saying is. Such things are learnt when one is young, as one learns to walk".

Chellaya looked out over the old man's head to the lagoon.

Another fisherman was stealing along in the water ready for the cast. Ah, swish out flew the net. No, nothing – yes, O joy, a gleam of silver in the meshes. Chellaya made up his mind suddenly.

"Now, look here, fellow, tell me this; could you teach me to cast a net?"

The old man covered his mouth with his hand, for it is not seemly that a fisher should smile in the presence of a Brahman.

"The lord is laughing at me," he said respectfully.

"I am not laughing, fellow. I have made a vow to Muniyappa that if he would take away the curse which he laid upon my son's child I would cast a net nightly in the lagoon. Now my son's child is well. Therefore if you will take me tomorrow night to a spot where no one will see us and bring me a net and teach me to cast it, I will give you five measures of rice. And if you speak a word of this to anyone, I will call down upon your head and your child's head ten thousand curses of Muniyappa",.

It is dangerous to risk being cursed by a Brahman, so the fisherman agreed and next evening took Chellaya to a bay in the lagoon and showed him how to cast the net. For an hour Chellaya waded about in the shallow water experiencing a dreadful pleasure. Every moment he glanced over his shoulder to the land to make sure that nobody was in sight; every moment came the pang that he was the first Brahman to pollute his caste by fishing; and every moment came the keen joy of hope that this time the net would swish out and fall in a gentle circle upon a silver fish.

Chellaya caught nothing that night, but he had gone too far to turn back. He gave the fisherman two rupees for the net, and hid it under a rock, and every night he went away to the solitary creek; made a little pile of his white Brahman clothes on the sand, and stepped into the shallow water with his net. There he fished until the sun sank. And sometimes now he caught fish which very reluctantly he had to throw back into the water, for he was afraid to carry them back to his wife.

Very soon a strange rumour began to spread in the town that the Brahman Chellaya had polluted his caste by fishing. At first people would not believe it; such a thing could not happen, for it had never happened before. But at last so many people told the story, – and one man had seen Chellaya carrying a net and another had seen him wading in the lagoon – that everyone began to believe it, the lower castes with great pleasure and the Brahmans with great shame and anger.

Hardly had people begun to believe this rumour than an almost stranger thing began to be talked of. The Brahman Chittampalam, who was Chetlaya's neighbour, had polluted his caste, it was said, by carrying earth on his head. And this rumour also was true and it happened in this way.

Chittampalam was a taciturn man and a miser. If

The Two Brahmans

his thin scraggy wife used three chillies, where she might have done with two for the curry, he beat her soundly. About the time that Chellaya began to fish in secret, the water in Chittampalam's well began to grow brackish. It became necessary to dig a new well in the compound, but to dig a well means paying a lower caste man to do the work; for the earth that is taken out has to be carried away on the head, and it is pollution for a Brahman to carry earth on his head. So Chittampalam sat in his compound thinking for many days how to avoid paying a man to dig a new well: and meanwhile the taste of the water from the old well became more and more unpleasant. At last it became impossible even for Chittampalam's wife to drink the water; there was only one way out of it; a new well must be dug and he could not bring himself to pay for the digging: he must dig the well himself. So every night for a week Chittampalam went down to the darkest corner of his compound and dug a well and carried earth on his head and thereby polluted his caste.

The other Brahmans were enraged with Chellaya and Chittampalam and, after abusing them and calling them pariahs, they cast them out for ever from the Brahman caste and refused to eat or drink with them or to talk to them; and they took an oath that their children's children should never marry with the grandsons and granddaughters of Chellaya and Chittampalam. But if people of other castes talked to them of the matter, they denied all knowledge of it and swore that no Brahman had ever caught fish or carried earth on his head. Chittampalam was not much concerned at the anger of the

Brahmans, for he had saved the hire of a well-digger and he had never taken pleasure in the conversation of other Brahmans and, besides, he shortly after died.

Chellaya, being a small fat man and of a more pleasant and therefore more sensitive nature, felt his sin and the disapproval of his friends deeply. For some days he gave up his fishing, but they were weary days to him and he gained nothing, for the Brahmans still refused to talk to him. All day long in the temple and in his compound he sat and thought of his evenings when he waded in the blue waters of the lagoon, and of the little islands resting like plumes of smoke or feathers upon the sky, and of the line of pink flamingoes like thin posts at regular intervals set to mark a channel, and of the silver gleam of darting fish. In the evening, when he knew the fishermen were taking out their nets, his longing became intolerable: he dared not go down to the lagoon for he knew that his desire would master him. So for five nights he sat in his compound, and, as the saying is, his fat went off in desire. On the sixth night he could stand it no longer; once more he polluted his caste by catching fish.

After this Chellaya no longer tried to struggle against himself but continued to fish until at the age of fifty he died. Then, as time went on, the people who had known Chellaya and Chittampalam died too, and the story of how each had polluted his caste began to be forgotten. Only it was known in Yalpanam that no Brahman could marry into those two families, because there was something wrong with

The Two Brahmans

their caste. Some said that Chellaya had carried earth on his head and that Chittampalam had caught fish; in any case the descendants of Chellaya and Chittampalam had to go to distant villages to find Brahman wives and husbands for their sons and daughters.

Chellaya's hut and Chittampalam's hut still stand where they stood under the coconut trees by the side of the lagoon, and in one lives Chellaya, the great-great-great-grandson of Chellaya who caught fish, and in the other Chittampalam the great-great-great-grandson of Chittampalam who carried earth on his head. Chittampalam has a very beautiful daughter and Chellaya has one son unmarried. Now this son saw Chittampalam's daughter by accident through the fence of the compound, and he went to his father and said :

"They say that our neighbour's daughter will have a big dowry; should we not make a proposal of marriage'?"

The father had often thought of marrying his son to Chittampalam's daughter, not because he had seen her through the compound fence but because he had reason to believe that her dowry would be large. But he had never mentioned it to his wife or to his son, because he knew that it, was said that an ancestor of Chittampalam had once dug a well and carried earth on his head. Now however that his son himself suggested the marriage, he approved of the idea, and, as the custom is, told his wife to go to Chittampalam's house and look at the girl. So his wife went formally to Chittampalam's house for the visit preparatory to an offer of marriage, and she came back and reported that the girl was beautiful and fit for even her son to marry.

Chittampalam had himself often thought of proposing to Chellaya that Chellaya's son should marry his daughter, but he had been ashamed to do this because he knew that Chellaya's ancestor had caught fish and thereby polluted his caste. Otherwise the match was desirable, for he would be saved from all the trouble of finding a husband for her in some distant village. However, if Chellaya himself proposed it, he made up his mind not to put any difficulties in the way. The next time that the two met, Chellaya made the proposal and Chittampalam accepted it and then they went back to Chellaya's compound to discuss the question of dowry. As is usual in such cases the father of the girl wants the dowry to be small and the father of the boy wants it to be large, and all sorts of reasons are given on both sides why it should be small or large, and the argument begins to grow warm. The argument became so warm that at last Chittampalam lost his temper and said:

"One thousand rupees! Is that what you want? Why, a fisher should take the girl with no dowry at all!"

"Fisher!" shouted Chellaya. "Who would marry into the pariah caste, that defiles itself by digging wells and carrying earth on its head? You had better give two thousand rupees to a pariah to take your daughter out of your house".

"Fisher! Low caste dog!" shouted Chittampalam.

"Pariah!" screamed Chellaya.

The Two Brahmans

Chittampalam rushed from the compound and for many days the two Brahmans refused to talk a word to one another. At last Chellaya's son, who had again seen the daughter of Chittampalam through the fence of the compound, talked to his father and then to Chittampalam, and the quarrel was healed and they began to discuss again the question of dowry. But the old words rankled and they were still sore, as soon as the discussion began to grow warm it ended once more by their calling each other "Fisher" and "Pariah". The same thing has happened now several times, and Chittampalam is beginning to think of going to distant villages to find a husband for his daughter. Chellaya's son is very unhappy; he goes down every evening and sits by the waters of the blue lagoon on the very spot where his great-great-great-grandfather Chellaya used to sit and watch the fishermen cast their nets.

Pearls and Swine

I had finished my hundred up – or rather he had – with the Colonel and we strolled into the smoking room for a smoke and a drink round the fire before turning in. There were three other men already round the fire and they widened their circle to take us in. I didn't know them, hadn't spoken to them or indeed to anyone except the Colonel in the large gaudy uncomfortably comfortable hotel. I was run down, out of sorts generally, and – like a fool, I thought now – had taken a week off to eat, or rather to read the menus of interminable table d'hôte dinners, to play golf and to walk on the "front" at Torquay.

I had only arrived the day before, but the Colonel (retired) a jolly tubby little man – with white moustaches like two S's lying side by side on the top of his stupid red lips and his kind choleric eyes bulging out on a life which he was quite content never for a moment to understand – made it a point, my dear Sir, to know every new arrival within one hour after he arrived.

We got our drinks and as, rather forgetting that I was in England, I murmured the Eastern formula, I noticed vaguely one of the other three glance at me over his shoulder for a moment. The Colonel stuck out his fat little legs in front of him, turning up his neatly shoed toes before the blaze. Two of the others were talking, talking as men so often do in the comfortable chairs of smoking rooms between ten and eleven at night, earnestly, seriously, of what they call affairs, or politics or questions. I listened to their fat, full-fed assured voices in that heavy room which smelt of solidity, safety, horsehair furniture, tobacco smoke, and the faint civilized aroma of whisky and soda. It came as a shock to me in that atmosphere that they were discussing India and the East: it does you know every now and again. Sentimental? Well, I expect one is sentimental about it, having lived there. It doesn't seem to go with solidity and horsehair furniture: the fifteen years come back to one in one moment all in a heap. How one hated it and how one loved it!

I suppose they had started on the Durbar and the King's visit. They had got on to Indian unrest, to our position in India, its duties, responsibilities, to the problem of East and West. They hadn't been there of course, they hadn't even seen the brothel and café chantant at Port Said suddenly open out into that pink and blue desert that leads you through Africa and Asia into the heart of the East. But they knew all about it, they had solved, with their fat voices and in their fat heads, riddles, older than the Sphinx, of peoples remote and ancient and mysterious whom they had never seen and could never understand. One was, I imagine, a stock-jobber, plump and comfortable with a greasy forehead and a high colour in his cheeks, smooth shiny brown hair and a carefully grown small moustache: a good dealer in the market: sharp and confident, with a loud voice and shifty eyes. The other was a clergyman: need I say more? Except that he was more of a clergyman even than most clergymen, I mean that he wore tight things – leggings don't they call them? or breeches? – round his calves. I never know what it means: whether they are bishops or rural deans or archdeacons or archimandrites. In any case I mistrust them even more than the black trousers: they seem to close the last door for anything human to get in through the black clothes. The dog collar closes up the armour above, and below, as long as they *were* trousers, at any rate some whiff of humanity might have eddied up the legs of them and touched bare flesh. But the gaiters button them up finally, irremediably, for ever.

I expect he was an archdeacon; he was saying: "You can't impose Western civilization upon an Eastern people – I believe I'm right in saying that there are over two hundred millions in our Indian Empire – without a little disturbance. I'm a Liberal you know. I've been a Liberal my whole life – family tradition – though I grieve to say I could *not* follow Mr. Gladstone on the Home Rule question. It seems to me a good sign, this movement, an awakening among the people. But don't misunderstand me, my dear Sir; I am not making any excuses for the methods of the extremists. Apart from my calling – I have a natural horror of violence. Nothing can condone violence, the taking of human life, it's savagery, terrible, terrible".

"They don't put it down with a strong enough hand", the stock-jobber was saying almost fiercely. "There's too much Liberalism in the East, too much namby-pambyism. It is all right here, of course, but it's not suited to the East. They want a strong hand. After all they owe us something: we aren't going to take all the kicks and leave them all the halfpence. Rule' em, I say. rule 'em if you're going to rule 'em. Look after 'em, of course: give 'em schools, if they want education – schools, hospitals, roads, and railways. Stamp out the plague, fever, famine. But let 'em know we are top dog. That's the way to run an eastern country. I am a white man, you're black; I'll treat you well, give you courts and justice; but I'm the superior race, I'm master here".

The man who had looked round at me when I said "Here's luck!" was fidgeting about in his chair uneasily. I examined him more carefully. There was no mistaking the cause of his irritation It was written on his face, the small close-cut white moustache, the smooth firm cheeks with the red-and-brown glow on them, the innumerable wrinkles round the eyes, and above all the eyes themselves, that had grown slow and steady and unastonished, watching that inexplicable, meaningless march of life under blazing suns. He had seen it, he knew. "Ah", I thought. "he is beginning to feel his liver. If he would only begin to speak, we might have some fun".

"H'm, h'm", said the archdeacon. "Of course there's something in what you say. Slow and sure. Things may be going too fast, and, as I say, I'm entirely for putting down violence and illegality with a strong hand. And after all, my dear Sir, when you say we're the superior race you imply a duty. Even in secular matters we must spread the light. I believe – devoutly – I am not ashamed to say so – that we are. We're reaching the people there, it's the cause of the unrest, we set them an example. They

Pearls and Swine

desire to follow. Surely, surely we should help to guide their feet. I don't speak without a certain knowledge. I take a great interest, I may even say that I play my small part, in the work of one of our great missionary societies. I see our young men, many of them risen from the people, educated often, and highly educated (I venture to think), in Board Schools. I see them go out full of high ideals to live among those poor people. And I see them when they come back and tell me their tales honestly, unostentatiously. It is always the same, a message of hope and comfort. We are getting at the people, by example, by our lives, by our conduct. They respect us."

I heard a sort of groan. and then quite loud, these strange words:

"Kasimutal Rameswaranvaraiyil terintavan".

"I beg your pardon", said the Archdeacon, turning to the interrupter.

"I beg yours. Tamil, Tamil, proverb. Came into my mind. Spoke without thinking. Beg yours".

"Not at all. Very interesting. You've lived in India? Would you mind my asking you for a translation ?"

"It means 'he knows everything between Benares and Rameswaran'. Last time I heard it, an old Tamil, seventy or eighty years old, perhaps – he looked a hundred – used it of one of your young men. The young man, by the bye, had been a year and a half in India. D'you understand?"

"Well, I'm not sure I do: I've heard, of course, of Benares, – but Rameswaram, I don't seem to remember the name".

I laughed; I could not help it; the little Anglo-Indian looked so fierce. "Ah!" he said, "you don't recollect the name. Well, it's pretty famous out there. Great temple – Hindu – right at the southern tip of India. Benares, you know, is up north. The old Tamil meant that your friend knew everything in India after a year and a half: *he* didn't you know, after seventy, after seven thousand years. Perhaps you also don't recollect that the Tamils are Dravidians? They've been there since the beginning of time, before we came, or the Dutch or Portuguese or the Muhammadans, or our cousins, the other Aryans. Uncivilized, black? Perhaps, but, if they're black, after all it's *their* suns, through thousands of years, that have blackened them. They ought to know, if anyone does: but they don't, they don't pretend to. But you two gentlemen, you seem to know everything between Kasimutal – that's Benares – and Rameswaram, without having seen the sun at all".

"My dear sir', began the Archdeacon pompously, but the jobber interrupted him. He had had a number of whiskies and sodas, and was quite heated. "It's very easy to sneer: it doesn't mean because you've lived a few years in a place . . ."

"I? Thirty. But they – seven thousand at least".

"I say, it doesn't mean because you've lived thirty years in a place that you know all about it. Ramisram, or whatever the damned place is called, I've never heard of it and don't want to. You do, that's part of your job, I expect. But I read the papers, I've read books too, mind you, about India. I know what's going on. One knows enough –

enough – data: East and West and the difference: I can form an opinion – I've a right to it even if I've never heard of Ramis what d'you call it. You've lived there – and you can't see the wood for the trees. We see it because we're out of it – see it at a distance".

"Perhaps", said the Archdeacon "there's a little misunderstanding. The discussion – if I may say so – is getting a little heated – unnecessarily, I think. We hold our views. This gentleman has lived in the country. He holds others. I'm sure it would be most interesting to hear them. But I confess I didn't quite gather them from what he said".

The little man was silent: he sat back, his eyes fixed on the ceiling. Then he smiled.

"I won't give you views", he said. "But if you like I'll give you what you call details, things seen, facts. Then you can give me *your* views on 'em".

They murmured approval.

"Let's see, it's fifteen, seventeen years ago. I had a district then about as big as England. There may have been twenty Europeans in it, counting the missionaries, and twenty million Tamils and Telegus. I expect nineteen million of the Tamils and Telegus never saw a white man from one year's end to the other, or if they did, they caught a glimpse of me under a sun helmet riding through their village on a flea-bitten grey Indian mare. Well, Providence had so designed it that there was a stretch of coast in that district which was a barren wilderness of sand and scrubby thorn jungle – and nothing else – for three hundred miles; no towns, no villages, no water, just sand and trees for three hundred miles.

O, and sun, I forget that, blazing sun. And in the water off the shore at one place there were oysters, millions of them lying and breeding at the bottom, four or five fathoms down. And in the oysters, or some of them, were pearls.

Well, we rule India and the sea, so the sea belongs to us, and the oysters are in the sea and the pearls are in the oysters. Therefore of course the pearls belong to us. But they lie in five fathoms. How to get 'em up, that's the question. You'd think being progressive we'd dredge for them or send down divers in diving dresses. But we don't, not in India. They've been fishing up the oysters and the pearls there ever since the beginning of time, naked brown men diving feet first out of long wooden boats into the blue sea and sweeping the oysters off the bottom of the sea into baskets slung to their sides. They were doing it centuries and centuries before we came, when – as someone said – our ancestors were herding swine on the plains of Norway. The Arabs of the Persian Gulf came down in dhows and fished up pearls which found their way to Solomon and the Queen of Sheba. They still come, and the Tamils and Moormen of the district come, and they fish 'em up in the same way, diving out of long wooden boats shaped and rigged as in Solomon's time, as they were centuries before him and the Queen of Sheba. No difference, you see, except that we – Government I mean – take two-thirds of all the oysters fished up: the other third we give to the diver, Arab or Tamil or Moorman, for his trouble in fishing 'em up.

We used to have a Pearl Fishery about once in

three years. It lasted six weeks or two months just between the two monsoons, the only time the sea is calm there. And I had, of course, to go and superintend it, to take Government's share of oysters, to sell them, to keep order, to keep out K.D.'s – that means Known Depredators – and smallpox and cholera. We had what we called a camp, in the wilderness remember, on the hot sand down there by the sea: it sprang up in a night, a town, a big town of thirty or forty thousand people, a little India, Asia almost, even a bit of Africa. They came from all districts: Tamils, Telegus, fat Chetties, Parsees, Bombay merchants, Sinhalese from Ceylon, the Arabs and their negroes, Somalis probably, who used to be their slaves. It was an immense gamble; everyone bought oysters for the chance of the prizes in them: it would have taken fifty white men to superintend that camp properly: they gave me one, a little boy of twenty-four fresh-cheeked from England, just joined the service. He had views, he had been educated in a Board School, won prizes, scholarships, passed the Civil Service Exam. Yes, he had views; he used to explain them to me when he first arrived. He got some new ones I think before he got out of that camp. You'd say he only saw details, things happen, facts, data. Well, he did that too. He saw men die – he hadn't seen that in his Board School – die of plague or cholera, like flies, all over the place, under the trees, in the boats, outside the little door of his own little hut. And he saw flies, too, millions, billions of them all day long buzzing, crawling over everything, his hands, his little fresh face, his food. And he smelt the smell of millions of decaying oysters all day long and all night long for six weeks. He was sick four or five times a day for six weeks; the smell did that. Insanitary? Yes, very. Why is it allowed? The pearls, you see, the pearls: you must get them out of the oysters as you must get the oysters out of the sea. And the pearls are very often small and embedded in the oyster's body. So you put all the oysters, millions of them, in dug-out canoes in the sun to rot. They rot very well in that sun, and the flies come and lay eggs in them, and maggots come out of the eggs and more flies come out of the maggots; and between them all, the maggots and the sun, the oysters' bodies disappear, leaving the pearls and a little sand at the bottom of the canoe. Unscientific? Yes, perhaps; but after all it's our camp, our fishery – just as it was in Solomon's time? At any rate, you see, it's the East. But whatever it is, and whatever the reason, the result involves flies, millions of them and a smell, a stench – Lord! I can smell it now.

There was one other white man there. He was a planter, so he said, and he had come to "deal" in pearls. He dropped in on us out of a native boat at sunset on the second day. He had a red face and a red nose, he was unhealthily fat for the East: the whites of his eyes were rather blue and rather red: they were also watery.

I noticed that his hand shook, and that he first refused and then took a whisky and soda – a bad sign in the East. He wore very dirty white clothes and a vest instead of a shirt: he apparently had no baggage of any sort. But he was a white man, and so he ate with us that night and a good many nights afterwards.

In the second week he had his first attack of D.T. We pulled him through, Robson and I, in the intervals of watching over the oysters. When he hadn't got D.T., he talked: he was a great talker, he also had views. I used to sit in the evenings – they were rare – when the fleet of boats had got in early and the oysters had been divided, in front of my hut and listen to him and Robson settling India and Asia, Africa too probably. We sat there in our long chairs on the sand looking out over the purple sea, towards a sunset like blood shot with gold. Nothing moved or stirred except the flies which were going to sleep in a mustard tree close by; they hung in buzzing clusters, billions of them on the smooth leaves and little twigs: literally it was black with them. It looked as if the whole tree had suddenly broken out all over into some disease of living black currants. Even the sea seemed to move with an effort in the hot, still air; only now and again a little wave would lift itself up very slowly, very wearily, poise itself for a moment, and then fall with a weary little thud on the sand.

I used to watch them, I say, in the hot still air and the smell of dead oysters – it pushed up against your face like something solid – talking, talking in their long chairs, while the sweat stood out in little drops on their foreheads and trickled from time to time down their noses. There wasn't, I suppose, anything wrong with Robson, he was all right at bottom, but he annoyed me; irritated me in that smell. He was too cocksure altogether, of himself, of his Board School education, of life, of his 'views'. He was going to run India on new lines, laid down in some damned Manual of Political Science out of which they learn life in Board Schools and extension lectures. He would run his own life, I dare say, on the same lines, laid down in some other text book or primer. He hadn't seen anything, but he knew exactly what it was all like. There was nothing curious, astonishing, unexpected, in life, he was ready for any emergency. And we were all wrong, all on the wrong tack in dealing with natives! He annoyed me a little, you know, when the thermometer stood at 99, at 6 p.m., but what annoyed me still more was that they – the natives! – were all wrong too. They too had to be taught how to live – and die, too, I gathered.

But his views were interesting, very interesting – especially in the long chairs there under the immense Indian sky, with the camp at our hands – just as it had been in the time of Moses and Abraham – and behind us the jungle for miles, and behind that India, three hundred millions of them listening to the piping voice of a Board School boy; are the inferior race, these three hundred millions – mark race, though there are more races in India than people in Peckham – and we, of course, are superior. They've stopped somehow on the bottom rung of the ladder of which we've very nearly, if not quite, reached the top. They've stopped there hundreds, thousands of years: but it won't take any time to lead 'em up by the hand to our rung. It's to be done like this: by showing them that they're our brothers, inferior brothers; by reason, arguing them out of their superstitions, false beliefs; by education, by science, by example, yes, even he did not forget example, and White, sitting by his side with his red nose and watery eyes, nodded approval. And all this must be done scientifically, logically, systematically: if it were, a Commissioner could revolutionize a province in five years, turn it into a Japanese India, with all the ryots as well as all the vakils and students running up the ladder of European civilization to become, I suppose, glorified Board School angels at the top. "But you've none of you got clear plans out here", he piped, "you never work on any system; you've got no point of view. The result is" – here, I think, he was inspired, by the dead oysters, perhaps – "instead of getting hold of the East, it's the East which gets hold of you".

And White agreed with him, solemnly, at any rate when he was sane and sober. And I couldn't complain of his inexperience. He was rather reticent at first, but afterwards we heard much – too much – of his experiences – one does, when a man gets D.T. He said he was a gentleman, and I believe it was true: he had been to a public school: Cheltenham or Repton. He hadn't, I gathered, succeeded as a gentleman at home, so they sent him to travel in the East. He liked it, it suited him. So he became a planter in Assam. That was fifteen years ago, but he didn't like Assam: the luck was against him – it always was – and he began to roll; and when a man starts rolling in India, well – He had been a clerk in merchants' offices; he had served in a draper's shop in Calcutta; but the luck was always against him.

Then he tramped up and down India, through Ceylon, Burma; he had got at one time or another to the Malay States and when he was very bad one day, he talked of cultivating camphor in Java. He had been a sailor on a coasting tramp; he had sold horses (which didn't belong to him) in the Deccan somewhere; he had tramped day after day begging his way for months in native bazaars; he had lived for six months with, and on, a Tamil. woman in some little village down in the south. Now he was 'dealing in' pearls. "India's got hold of me", he'd say, "India's got hold of me and the East".

He had views too, very much like Robson's, with additions. 'The strong hand' came in, and 'rule'. We ought to govern India more; we didn't now. Why, he had been in hundreds of places where he was the first Englishman that the people had ever seen. (Lord! think of that!). He talked a great deal about the hidden wealth of India and exploitation. He knew places where there was gold – workable too – only one wanted a little capital – coal probably and iron – and then there was this new stuff, radium. But we weren't go-ahead, progressive. the Government always put difficulties in his way. They made 'the native' their stalking-horse against European enterprise. He would work for the good of the native, he'd treat him firmly but kindly – especially, I thought, the native women, for his teeth were sharp and pointed and there were spaces between each, and there was something about his chin and jaw – *you* know the type, I expect.

As the fishing went on we had less time to talk. We had to work. The divers go out in the fleet of

Pearls and Swine

three hundred or four hundred boats every night and dive until midday. Then they sail back from the pearl banks and bring all their oysters into an immense Government enclosure where the Government share is taken. If the wind is favourable all the boats get back by 6 p.m. and the work is over at 7. But if the wind starts blowing off shore the fleet gets scattered and boats drop in one by one all night long. Robson and I had to be in the enclosure as long as there was a boat out, ready to see that, as soon as it did get in, the oysters were brought to the enclosure and Government got its share.

Well, the wind never did blow favourably that year. I sat in that enclosure sometimes for forty-eight hours on end. Robson found managing it rather difficult, so he didn't like to be left there alone. If you get two thousand Arabs, Tamils, Negroes, and Moormen, each with a bag .or two of oysters, into an enclosure a hundred and fifty yards by a hundred and fifty yards, and you only have thirty timid native 'subordinates' and twelve native policemen to control them – well, somehow or other he found a difficulty in applying his system of reasoning to them. The first time he tried it, we very nearly had a riot; it arose from a dispute between some Arabs and Tamils over the ownership of three oysters which fell out of a bag. The Arabs didn't understand Tamil, and the Tamils didn't understand Arabic, and, when I got down there, fetched by a frightened constable, there were sixty or seventy men fighting with great poles – they had pulled up the fence of the enclosure for weapons – and on the outskirts was Robson running round like a distracted hen with a white face and tears in his blue eyes. When we got the combatants separated, they had only killed one Tamil and broken nine or ten heads. Robson was very upset by that dead Tamil, he broke down utterly for a minute or two, I'm afraid.

Then White got his second attack. He was very bad: he wanted to kill himself, but what was worse than that, before killing himself, he wanted to kill other people. I hadn't been to bed for two nights and I knew I should have to sit up another night in that enclosure as the wind was all wrong again. I had given White a bed in my hut: it wasn't good to let him wander in the bazaar. Robson came down with a white face to tell me he had 'gone mad up there again.' I had to knock him down with the butt end of a rifle; he was a big man and I hadn't slept for forty eight hours, and then there were the flies and the smell of those dead oysters.

It sounds unreal, perhaps a nightmare, all this told here to you behind blinds and windows in this – " he sniffed – "in this smell of – of – horsehair furniture and paint and varnish. The curious thing is it didn't seem a nightmare out there. It was too real. Things happened, anything might happen, without shocking or astonishing. One just did one's work, hour after hour, keeping things going in that sun which stung one's bare hands, took the skin off even my face, among the flies and the smell. It wasn't a nightmare, it was just a few thousand Arabs and Indians fishing up oysters from the bottom of the sea. It wasn't even new, one felt it was old, old as the Bible, old as Adam, so the Arabs said. One hadn't much time to think, but one felt it and watched it, watched the things happen quietly, unastonished, as men do in the East. One does one's work, – forty eight hours at a stretch doesn't leave one much time or inclination for thinking, – waiting for things to happen. If you can prevent people from killing one another or robbing one another, or burning down the camp, or getting cholera or plague or small-pox, and if one can manage to get one night's sleep in three, one is fairly satisfied; one doesn't much worry about having to knock a mad gentleman from Repton on the head with the butt end of a rifle between-whiles.

I expect that's just what Robson would call 'not getting hold of India but letting India get hold of you'. Well, I said I wouldn't give you views and I won't: I'm giving you facts: what I want, you know, too is to give you the feeling of facts out there. After all that is data for your views, isn't it? Things here *feel* so different; you seem so far from life, with windows and blinds and curtains always in between, and then nothing ever happens, you never wait for things to happen, never watch things happening here. You are always doing things somehow – Lord knows what they are – according I suppose to systems, views, opinions. But out there you live so near to life, every morning you smell damp earth if you splash too much in your tin bath. And things happen slowly, inexorably by fate, and you – you don't do things, you watch with the three hundred millions. You feel it there in everything, even in the sunrise and sunset, every day, the immensity, inexorableness, mystery of things happening. You feel the whole earth waking up or going to sleep in a great arch of sky; you feel small, not very powerful. But who ever felt the sun set or rise in London or Torquay either? It doesn't: you just turn on or turn off the electric light.

White was very bad that night. When he recovered from being knocked down by the rifle, I had to tie him down to the bed. And then Robson broke down – nerves, you know. I had to go back to the enclosure and I wanted him to stay and look after White in the hut – it wasn't safe to leave him alone even tied down with cord to the camp bed. But this was apparently another emergency to which the manual system did not apply. He couldn't face it alone in the hut with that man tied to the bed. White was certainly not a pretty sight writhing about there, and his face – have you ever seen a man in the last stages of D.T? I beg your pardon. I suppose you haven't. It isn't nice, and White was also seeing things, not nice either: not snakes you know as people do in novels when they get D.T., but things which had happened to him, and things which he had done – they weren't nice either – and curious ordinary things distorted in a most unpleasant way. He was very much troubled by snipe: hundreds of them kept on rising out of the bed from beside him with that shrill 'cheep! cheep!' of theirs: he felt their soft little feathered bodies against his bare skin as they fluttered up from under him somewhere and flew out of the window. It threw him into paroxysms of fear, agonies: it made one, I admit, feel chilly round the heart to hear him pray one to stop it .

And Robson was also not a nice sight. I hate seeing a sane man break down with fear, mere abject fear. He just sat down at last on a cane-bottomed chair and cried like a baby. Well, that did him some good, but he wasn't fit to be left alone with White. I had to take White down to the enclosure, and I tied him to a post with coir rope near the table at which I sat there. There was nothing else to do. And Robson came too and sat there at my side through the night watching White, terrified but fascinated.

Can you picture that enclosure to yourself down on the sandy shore with its great fence of rough poles cut in the jungle, lighted by a few flares, torches dipped in coconut oil: and the white man tied to a pole raving, writhing in the flickering light which just showed too Robson's white scared little face? And in the intervals of taking over oysters and settling disputes between Arabs and Somalis and Tamils and Moormen, sat at the table writing a report (which had to go by runner next morning) on a proposal to introduce the teaching of French in 'English schools' in towns. That wasn't a very good report. White gave us the whole history of his life between ten p.m. and four a.m. in the morning. He didn't leave much to the imagination; a parson would have said that in that hour the memory of his sins came upon him – O, I beg your pardon. But really I think they did. I thought I had lived long enough out there to have heard without a shock anything that men can do and do do – especially white men who have 'gone under.' But I hadn't: I couldn't stomach the story of White's life told by himself. It wasn't only that he had robbed and swindled himself through India up and down for fifteen years. That was bad enough for there wasn't a station where he hadn't swindled and bamboozled his fellow white men. But it was what he had done when he got away 'among the natives' – to men, and women too, away from civilization, in the jungle villages and high up in the mountains. God! the cold, civilized. corrupted cruelty of it. I told you, I think, that his teeth were pointed and spaced out in his mouth.

And his remorse was the most horrible thing, tied to that post there, writhing under the flickering light of the flare: the remorse of fear – fear of punishment, of what was coming, of death, of the horrors, real horrors and the phantom horrors of madness.

Often during the night there was nothing to be heard in the enclosure but his screams, curses, hoarse whispers of fear. We seemed alone there in the vast stillness of the sky: only now and then a little splash from the sea down on the shore. And then would come a confused murmur from the sea and a little later perhaps the wailing voice of one man calling to another from boat to boat across the water "Abdulla! Abdulla!" And I would go out on to the shore. There were boats, ten, fifteen, twenty, perhaps, coming in from the banks, sad, mysterious, in the moonlight, gliding in with the little splashings of the great round oars. Except for the slow moving of the oars one would have thought they were full of the dead, there was not a movement on board, until the boats touched the sand. Then the dark shadows, which lay like dead men about the boats, would leap into life – there would rise a sudden din of hoarse voices, shouting, calling, quarrelling. The boats swarmed with shadows running about, gesticulating, staggering under sacks of oysters, dropping one after the other over the boats' sides into the sea, The sea was full of them and soon the shore too, Arabs, Negroes, Tamils, bowed under the weight of the sacks. They came up dripping from the sea. They burst with a roar into the enclosure; they flung down their sacks of oysters with a crash. The place was full of swaying struggling forms: of men calling to one another in their different tongues: of the smell of the sea.

And above everything one could hear the screams and prayers of the madman writhing at the post. They gathered about him, stared at him. The light of the flares fell on their dark faces, shining and dripping from the sea. They looked calm, impassive, stern. It shone too on the circle of eyes: one saw the whites of them all round him: they seemed to be judging him, weighing him: calm patient eyes of men who watched unastonished the procession of things. The Tamils' squat black figures nearly naked watched him silently, almost carelessly. The Arabs in their long dirty night-shirts, black-bearded, discussed him earnestly together with their guttural voices. Only an enormous negro, towering up to six feet six at least above the crowd, dressed in sacks and an enormous ulster. with ten copper coffee pots slung over his back and a pipe made of a whole coconut with an iron tube stuck in it in his hand, stood smiling mysteriously.

www.classictravelbooks.com

And White thought they weren't real, that they were devils of Hell sent to plague and torture him. He cursed them, whispered at them, howled with fear. I had to explain to them that the Sahib was not well, that the sun had touched him, that they must move away. They understood. They salaamed quietly, and moved away slowly, dignified.

I don't know how many times this didn't happen during the night. But towards morning White began to grow very weak. He moaned perpetually. Then he began to be troubled by the flesh. As dawn showed grey in the east, he was suddenly shaken by convulsions horrible to see. He screamed for someone to bring him a woman and, as he screamed, his head fell back: he was dead. I cut the cords quickly in a terror of haste, and covered the horror of the face. Robson was sitting in a heap in his chair. He was sobbing, his face in his hands.

At that moment I was told I was wanted on the shore. I went quickly. The sea looked cold and grey under the faint light from the East. A cold little wind just ruffled the surface of the water. A solitary boat stood out black against the sky, just throbbing slowly up and down on the water close in shore. They had a dead Arab on board, he had died suddenly while diving, they wanted my permission to bring the body ashore. Four men waded out to the boat: the corpse was lifted out and placed upon their shoulders. They waded back slowly: the feet of the dead man stuck out, toes pointing up, very stark, over the shoulders of the men in front. The body was laid on the sand. The bearded face of the dead man looked very calm, very dignified in the faint light. An Arab, his brother, sat down. upon the sand near his head. He covered himself with sackcloth. I heard him weeping. It was very silent, very cold and still on the shore in the early dawn.

A tall figure stepped forward, it was the Arab sheik, the leader of the boat. He laid his hand on the head of the weeping man and spoke to him calmly, eloquently, compassionately. I didn't understand Arabic, but I could understand what he was saying. The dead man had lived, had worked, had died. He had died working, without suffering, as men should desire to die. He had left a son behind him. The speech went on calmly, eloquently, I heard continually the word Khallas – all is over, finished. I watched the figures outlined against the grey sky – the long lean outline of the corpse with the toes sticking up so straight and stark, the crouching huddled figure of the weeping man and the tall upright sheik standing by his side. They were motionless, sombre, mysterious, part of the grey sea, of the grey sky.

Suddenly the dawn broke red in the sky. The sheik stopped, motioned silently to the four men. They lifted the dead man on to their shoulders. They moved away down the shore by the side of the sea which began to stir under the cold wind. By their side walked the sheik, his hand laid gently on the brother's arm. I watched them move away, silent, dignified. And over the shoulders of the men I saw the feet of the dead man with the toes sticking up straight and stark.

Then I moved away too, to make arrangements for White's burial: it had to be done at once ..

* * * * * * *

There was silence in the smoking-room. I looked round. The Colonel had fallen asleep with his mouth open. The jobber tried to look bored, the Archdeacon was, apparently, rather put out.

"It's too late, I think", said the Archdeacon, "to – Dear me; dear me, past one o'clock". He got up. "Don't you think you've chosen rather exceptional circumstances, out of the ordinary case?"

The Commissioner was looking into the few red coals that were all that was left of the fire.

"There's another Tamil proverb", he said: "When the cat puts his head into a pot, he thinks all is darkness."

Short Biography of Leonard Woolf

Christopher Ondaatje

Leonard Woolf was born in London in 1880. He spent five years at Trinity College, Cambridge – probably the most formative of his life – where he began lasting friendships with men like Lytton Strachey, E.M. Forster and John Maynard Keynes. In 1904, Woolf applied to join the home civil service but failed the exam. Instead, he was sent to Ceylon (now Sri Lanka) as a cadet in the Ceylon Civil Service. He remained there for nearly seven years. His resignation from the Ceylon civil service was formally accepted on 7 May 1912 and he married Virginia Stephen a few months later on 10 August. In November his first novel *The Village in the Jungle* was published, and a second novel *The Wise Virgins* was published in 1914. *Stories of the East* was first published in 1921.

Our Current List of Titles

Abdullah, Morag Mary, *My Khyber Marriage* - Morag Murray departed on a lifetime of adventure when she met and fell in love with Sirdar Ikbal Ali Shah, the son of an Afghan warlord. Leaving the comforts of her middle-class home in Scotland, Morag followed her husband into a Central Asia still largely unchanged since the 19th century.

Abernathy, Miles, *Ride the Wind* – the amazing true story of the little Abernathy Boys, who made a series of astonishing journeys in the United States, starting in 1909 when they were aged five and nine!

Beard, John, *Saddles East* – John Beard determined as a child that he wanted to see the Wild West from the back of a horse after a visit to Cody's legendary Wild West show. Yet it was only in 1948 – more than sixty years after seeing the flamboyant American showman – that Beard and his wife Lulu finally set off to follow their dreams.

Beker, Ana, *The Courage to Ride* – Determined to out-do Tschiffely, Beker made a 17,000 mile mounted odyssey across the Americas in the late 1940s that would fix her place in the annals of equestrian travel history.

Bey, A. M. Hassanein, *The Lost Oases* - At the dawning of the 20th century the vast desert of Libya remained one of last unexplored places on Earth. Sir Hassanein Bey, the dashing Egyptian diplomat turned explorer, befriended the Muslim leaders of the elusive Senussi Brotherhood who controlled the deserts further on, and became aware of rumours of a "lost oasis" which lay even deeper in the desert. In 1923 the explorer led a small caravan on a remarkable seven month journey across the centre of Libya.

Bird, Isabella, *Among the Tibetans* – A rousing 1889 adventure, an enchanting travelogue, a forgotten peek at a mountain kingdom swept away by the waves of time.

www.classictravelbooks.com

Bird, Isabella, *On Horseback* in *Hawaii* – The Victorian explorer's first horseback journey, in which she learns to ride astride, in early 1873.

Bird, Isabella, *Journeys in Persia and Kurdistan, Volumes 1 and 2* – The intrepid Englishwoman undertakes another gruelling journey in 1890.

Bird, Isabella, *A Lady's Life in the Rocky Mountains* – The story of Isabella Bird's adventures during the winter of 1873 when she explored the magnificent unspoiled wilderness of Colorado. Truly a classic.

Bird, Isabella, *Unbeaten Tracks in Japan, Volumes One and Two* – A 600-mile solo ride through Japan undertaken by the intrepid British traveller in 1878.

Blackmore, Charles, *In the Footsteps of Lawrence of Arabia* - In February 1985, fifty years after T. E. Lawrence was killed in a motor bicycle accident in Dorset, Captain Charles Blackmore and three others of the Royal Green Jackets Regiment set out to retrace Lawrence's exploits in the Arab Revolt during the First World War. They spent twenty-nine days with meagre supplies and under extreme conditions, riding and walking to the source of the Lawrence legend.

Boniface, Lieutenant Jonathan, *The Cavalry Horse and his Pack* – Quite simply the most important book ever written in the English language by a military man on the subject of equestrian travel.

Bosanquet, Mary, *Saddlebags for Suitcases* – In 1939 Bosanquet set out to ride from Vancouver, Canada, to New York. Along the way she was wooed by love-struck cowboys, chased by a grizzly bear and even suspected of being a Nazi spy, scouting out Canada in preparation for a German invasion. A truly delightful book.

de Bourboulon, Catherine, *Shanghai à Moscou (French)* – the story of how a young Scottish woman and

Other Titles

her aristocratic French husband travelled overland from Shanghai to Moscow in the late 19th Century.

Brown, Donald; *Journey from the Arctic* – A truly remarkable account of how Brown, his Danish companion and their two trusty horses attempt the impossible, to cross the silent Arctic plateaus, thread their way through the giant Swedish forests, and finally discover a passage around the treacherous Norwegian marshes.

Bruce, Clarence Dalrymple, *In the Hoofprints of Marco Polo* – The author made a dangerous journey from Srinagar to Peking in 1905, mounted on a trusty 13-hand Kashmiri pony, then wrote this wonderful book.

Burnaby, Frederick; *A Ride to Khiva* – Burnaby fills every page with a memorable cast of characters, including hard-riding Cossacks, nomadic Tartars, vodka-guzzling sleigh-drivers and a legion of peasant ruffians.

Burnaby, Frederick, *On Horseback through Asia Minor* – Armed with a rifle, a small stock of medicines, and a single faithful servant, the equestrian traveler rode through a hotbed of intrigue and high adventure in wild inhospitable country, encountering Kurds, Circassians, Armenians, and Persian pashas.

Carter, General William, *Horses, Saddles and Bridles* – This book covers a wide range of topics including basic training of the horse and care of its equipment. It also provides a fascinating look back into equestrian travel history.

Cayley, George, *Bridle Roads of Spain* – Truly one of the greatest equestrian travel accounts of the 19th Century.

Chase, J. Smeaton, *California Coast Trails* – This classic book describes the author's journey from Mexico to Oregon along the coast of California in the 1890s.

Chase, J. Smeaton, *California Desert Trails* – Famous British naturalist J. Smeaton Chase mounted up and rode into the Mojave Desert to undertake the longest equestrian study of its kind in modern history.

Chitty, Susan, and Hinde, Thomas, *The Great Donkey Walk* - When biographer Susan Chitty and her novelist husband, Thomas Hinde, decided it was time to embark on a family adventure, they did it in style. In Santiago they bought two donkeys whom they named Hannibal and Hamilcar. Their two small daughters, Miranda (7) and Jessica (3) were to ride Hamilcar. Hannibal, meanwhile, carried the baggage. The walk they planned to undertake was nothing short of the breadth of southern Europe.

Christian, Glynn, *Fragile Paradise: The discovery of Fletcher Christian, "Bounty" Mutineer* - the great-great-great-great-grandson of the *Bounty* mutineer brings to life a fascinating and complex character history has portrayed as both hero and villain, and the real story behind a mutiny that continues to divide opinion more than 200 years later. The result is a brilliant and compelling historical detective story, full of intrigue, jealousy, revenge and adventure on the high seas.

Clark, Leonard, *Marching Wind, The* - The panoramic story of a mounted exploration in the remote and savage heart of Asia, a place where adventure, danger, and intrigue were the daily backdrop to wild tribesman and equestrian exploits.

Clark, Leonard, *A Wanderer Till I Die* - In a world with lax passport control, no airlines, and few rules, the young man from San Francisco floats effortlessly from one adventure to the next. When he's not drinking whiskey at the Raffles Hotel or listening to the "St. Louis Blues" on the phonograph in the jungle, he's searching for Malaysian treasure, being captured by Toradja head-hunters, interrogated by Japanese intelligence officers and lured into shady deals by European gun-runners.

Other Titles

Cobbett, William, *Rural Rides, Volumes 1 and 2* – In the early 1820s Cobbett set out on horseback to make a series of personal tours through the English countryside. These books contain what many believe to be the best accounts of rural England ever written, and remain enduring classics.

Codman, John, *Winter Sketches from the Saddle* – This classic book was first published in 1888. It recommends riding for your health and describes the septuagenarian author's many equestrian journeys through New England during the winter of 1887 on his faithful mare, Fanny.

Cunninghame Graham, Jean, *Gaucho Laird* – A superbly readable biography of the author's famous great-uncle, Robert "Don Roberto" Cunninghame Graham.

Cunninghame Graham, Robert, *Horses of the Conquest* – The author uncovered manuscripts which had lain forgotten for centuries, and wrote this book, as he said, out of gratitude to the horses of Columbus and the Conquistadors who shaped history.

Cunninghame Graham, Robert, *Magreb-el-Acksa* – The thrilling tale of how "Don Roberto" was kidnapped in Morocco!

Cunninghame Graham, Robert, *Rodeo* – An omnibus of the finest work of the man they called "the uncrowned King of Scotland," edited by his friend Aimé Tschiffely.

Cunninghame Graham, Robert, *Tales of Horsemen* – Ten of the most beautifully-written equestrian stories ever set to paper.

Cunninghame Graham, Robert, *Vanished Arcadia* – This haunting story about the Jesuit missions in South America from 1550 to 1767 was the inspiration behind the best-selling film *The Mission*.

Daly, H.W., *Manual of Pack Transportation* – This book is the author's masterpiece. It contains a wealth of information on various pack saddles, ropes and equipment, how to secure every type of load imaginable and instructions on how to organize a pack train.

Dixie, Lady Florence, *Riding Across Patagonia* – When asked in 1879 why she wanted to travel to such an outlandish place as Patagonia, the author replied without hesitation that she was taking to the saddle in order to flee from the strict confines of polite Victorian society. This is the story of how the aristocrat successfully traded the perils of a London parlor for the wind-borne freedom of a wild Patagonian bronco.

Dodwell, Christina, *Beyond Siberia* – The intrepid author goes to Russia's Far East to join the reindeer-herding people in winter.

Dodwell, Christina, *An Explorer's Handbook* – The author tells you everything you want to know about travelling: how to find suitable pack animals, how to feed and shelter yourself. She also has sensible and entertaining advice about dealing with unwanted visitors and the inevitable bureaucrats.

Dodwell, Christina, *Madagascar Travels* – Christina explores the hidden corners of this amazing island and, as usual, makes friends with its people.

Dodwell, Christina, *A Traveller in China* – The author sets off alone across China, starting with a horse and then transferring to an inflatable canoe.

Dodwell, Christina, *A Traveller on Horseback* – Christina Dodwell rides through Eastern Turkey and Iran in the late 1980s. The Sunday Telegraph wrote of the author's "courage and insatiable wanderlust," and in this book she demonstrates her gift for communicating her zest for adventure.

Dodwell, Christina, *Travels in Papua New Guinea* – Christina Dodwell spends two years exploring an island little known to the outside world. She travelled by foot, horse and dugout canoe among the Stone-Age tribes.

www.classictravelbooks.com

Other Titles

Dodwell, Christina, *Travels with Fortune* – the truly amazing account of the courageous author's first journey – a three-year odyssey around Africa by Landrover, bus, lorry, horse, camel, and dugout canoe!

Dodwell, Christina, *Travels with Pegasus* – This time Christina takes to the air! This is the story of her unconventional journey across North Africa in a microlight!

Duncan, John, *Travels in Western Africa in 1845 and 1846* - The author, a Lifeguardsman from Scotland, tells the hair-raising tale of his two journeys to what is now Benin. Sadly, Duncan has been forgotten until today, and we are proud to get this book back into print.

Ehlers, Otto, *Im Sattel durch die Fürstenhöfe Indiens* – In June 1890 the young German adventurer, Ehlers, lay very ill. His doctor gave him a choice: either go home to Germany or travel to Kashmir. So of course the Long Rider chose the latter. This is a thrilling yet humorous book about the author's adventures.

Farson, Negley, *Caucasian Journey* – A thrilling account of a dangerous equestrian journey made in 1929, this is an amply illustrated adventure classic.

Fox, Ernest, *Travels in Afghanistan* – The thrilling tale of a 1937 journey through the mountains, valleys, and deserts of this forbidden realm, including visits to such fabled places as the medieval city of Heart, the towering Hindu Kush mountains, and the legendary Khyber Pass.

Gall, Sandy, *Afghanistan – Agony of a Nation* - Sandy Gall has made three trips to Afghanistan to report the war there: in 1982, 1984 and again in 1986. This book is an account of his last journey and what he found. He chose to revisit the man he believes is the outstanding commander in Afghanistan: Ahmed Shah Masud, a dashing Tajik who is trying to organise resistance to the Russians on a regional, and eventually national scale.

www.classictravelbooks.com

Gall, Sandy, *Behind Russian Lines* - In the summer of 1982, Sandy Gall set off for Afghanistan on what turned out to be the hardest assignment of his life. During his career as a reporter he had covered plenty of wars and revolutions before, but this was the first time he had been required to walk all the way to an assignment and all the way back again, dodging Russian bombs *en route*.

Gallard, Babette, *Riding the Milky Way* - An essential guide to anyone planning to ride the ancient pilgrimage route to Santiago di Compostella, and a highly readable story for armchair travellers.

Galton, Francis, *The Art of Travel* – Originally published in 1855, this book became an instant classic and was used by a host of now-famous explorers, including Sir Richard Francis Burton of Mecca fame. Readers can learn how to ride horses, handle elephants, avoid cobras, pull teeth, find water in a desert, and construct a sleeping bag out of fur.

Glazier, Willard, *Ocean to Ocean on Horseback* – This book about the author's journey from New York to the Pacific in 1875 contains every kind of mounted adventure imaginable. Amply illustrated with pen and ink drawings of the time, the book remains a timeless equestrian adventure classic.

Goodwin, Joseph, *Through Mexico on Horseback* – The author and his companion, Robert Horiguichi, the sophisticated, multi-lingual son of an imperial Japanese diplomat, set out in 1931 to cross Mexico. They were totally unprepared for the deserts, quicksand and brigands they were to encounter during their adventure.

Hanbury-Tenison, Marika, *For Better, For Worse* – The author, an excellent story-teller, writes about her adventures visiting and living among the Indians of Central Brazil.

Other Titles

Hanbury-Tenison, Marika, *A Slice of Spice* – The fresh and vivid account of the author's hazardous journey to the Indonesian Islands with her husband, Robin.

Hanbury-Tenison, Robin, *Chinese Adventure* – The story of a unique journey in which the explorer Robin Hanbury-Tenison and his wife Louella rode on horseback alongside the Great Wall of China in 1986.

Hanbury-Tenison, Robin, *Fragile Eden* – The wonderful story of Robin and Louella Hanbury-Tenison's exploration of New Zealand on horseback in 1988. They rode alone together through what they describe as 'some of the most dramatic and exciting country we have ever seen.'

Hanbury-Tenison, Robin, *Mulu: The Rainforest* – This was the first popular book to bring to the world's attention the significance of the rain forests to our fragile ecosystem. It is a timely reminder of our need to preserve them for the future.

Hanbury-Tenison, Robin, *A Pattern of Peoples* – The author and his wife, Marika, spent three months travelling through Indonesia's outer islands and writes with his usual flair and sensitivity about the tribes he found there.

Hanbury-Tenison, Robin, *A Question of Survival* – This superb book played a hugely significant role in bringing the plight of Brazil's Indians to the world's attention.

Hanbury-Tenison, Robin, *The Rough and the Smooth* – The incredible story of two journeys in South America. Neither had been attempted before, and both were considered impossible!

Hanbury-Tenison, Robin, *Spanish Pilgrimage* – Robin and Louella Hanbury-Tenison went to Santiago de Compostela in a traditional way – riding on white horses over long-forgotten tracks. In the process they discovered more about the people and the country than

www.classictravelbooks.com

any conventional traveller would learn. Their adventures are vividly and entertainingly recounted in this delightful and highly readable book.

Hanbury-Tenison, Robin, *White Horses over France* – This enchanting book tells the story of a magical journey and how, in fulfilment of a personal dream, the first Camargue horses set foot on British soil in the late summer of 1984.

Hanbury-Tenison, Robin, *Worlds Apart – an Explorer's Life* – The author's battle to preserve the quality of life under threat from developers and machines infuses this autobiography with a passion and conviction which makes it impossible to put down.

Hanbury-Tenison, Robin, *Worlds Within – Reflections in the Sand* – This book is full of the adventure you would expect from a man of action like Robin Hanbury-Tenison. However, it is also filled with the type of rare knowledge that was revealed to other desert travellers like Lawrence, Doughty and Thesiger.

Haslund, Henning, *Mongolian Adventure* – An epic tale inhabited by a cast of characters no longer present in this lackluster world, shamans who set themselves on fire, rebel leaders who sacked towns, and wild horsemen whose ancestors conquered the world.

Heath, Frank, *Forty Million Hoofbeats* – Heath set out in 1925 to follow his dream of riding to all 48 of the Continental United States. The journey lasted more than two years, during which time Heath and his mare, Gypsy Queen, became inseparable companions.

Hinde, Thomas, *The Great Donkey Walk* -

Holt, William, *Ride a White Horse* – After rescuing a cart horse, Trigger, from slaughter and nursing him back to health, the 67-year-old Holt and his horse set out in 1964 on an incredible 9,000 mile, non-stop journey through western Europe.

www.classictravelbooks.com

Other Titles

Hopkins, Frank T., *Hidalgo and Other Stories* – For the first time in history, here are the collected writings of Frank T. Hopkins, the counterfeit cowboy whose endurance racing claims and Old West fantasies have polarized the equestrian world.

James, Jeremy, *Saddletramp* – The classic story of Jeremy James' journey from Turkey to Wales, on an unplanned route with an inaccurate compass, unreadable map and the unfailing aid of villagers who seemed to have as little sense of direction as he had.

James, Jeremy, *Vagabond* – The wonderful tale of the author's journey from Bulgaria to Berlin offers a refreshing, witty and often surprising view of Eastern Europe and the collapse of communism.

Jebb, Louisa, *By Desert Ways to Baghdad and Damascus* – From the pen of a gifted writer and intrepid traveller, this is one of the greatest equestrian travel books of all time.

Kluckhohn, Clyde, *To the Foot of the Rainbow* – This is not just a exciting true tale of equestrian adventure. It is a moving account of a young man's search for physical perfection in a desert world still untouched by the recently-born twentieth century.

Lambie, Thomas, *Boots and Saddles in Africa* – Lambie's story of his equestrian journeys is told with the grit and realism that marks a true classic.

Landor, Henry Savage, *In the Forbidden Land* – Illustrated with hundreds of photographs and drawings, this blood-chilling account of equestrian adventure makes for page-turning excitement.

Langlet, Valdemar, *Till Häst Genom Ryssland (Swedish)* – Denna reseskildring rymmer många ögonblicksbilder av möten med människor, från morgonbad med Lev Tolstoi till samtal med Tartarer och fotografering av fagra skördeflickor. Rikt illustrerad med foto och teckningar.

www.classictravelbooks.com

Leigh, Margaret, *My Kingdom for a Horse* – In the autumn of 1939 the author rode from Cornwall to Scotland, resulting in one of the most delightful equestrian journeys of the early twentieth century. This book is full of keen observations of a rural England that no longer exists.

Lester, Mary, *A Lady's Ride across Spanish Honduras in 1881* – This is a gem of a book, with a very entertaining account of Mary's vivid, day-to-day life in the saddle.

MacDermot, Brian, *Cult of the Sacred Spear* - here is that rarest of travel books, an exploration not only of a distant land but of a man's own heart. A confederation of pastoral people located in Southern Sudan and western Ethiopia, the Nuer warriors were famous for staging cattle raids against larger tribes and successfully resisted European colonization. Brian MacDermot, London stockbroker, entered into Nuer society as a stranger and emerged as Rial Nyang, an adopted member of the tribe. This book recounts this extraordinary emotional journey, regaling the reader with tales of pagan gods, warriors on mysterious missions, and finally the approach of warfare that continues to swirl across this part of Africa today.

Maillart, Ella, *Turkestan Solo* – A vivid account of a 1930s journey through this wonderful, mysterious and dangerous portion of the world, complete with its Kirghiz eagle hunters, lurking Soviet secret police, and the timeless nomads that still inhabited the desolate steppes of Central Asia.

Marcy, Randolph, *The Prairie Traveler* – There were a lot of things you packed into your saddlebags or the wagon before setting off to cross the North American wilderness in the 1850s. A gun and an axe were obvious necessities. Yet many pioneers were just as adamant about placing a copy of Captain Randolph Marcy's classic book close at hand.

Marsden, Kate, *Riding through Siberia: A Mounted Medical Mission in 1891* - This immensely readable book is a mixture of adventure, extreme hardship and compassion as the author travels the Great Siberian Post Road.

Marsh, Hippisley Cunliffe, *A Ride Through Islam* – A British officer rides through Persia and Afghanistan to India in 1873. Full of adventures, and with observant remarks on the local Turkoman equestrian traditions.

MacCann, William, *Viaje a Caballo* – Spanish-language edition of the British author's equestrian journey around Argentina in 1848.

Meline, James, *Two Thousand Miles on Horseback: Kansas to Santa Fé in 1866* – A beautifully written, eye witness account of a United States that is no more.

Muir Watson, Sharon, *The Colour of Courage* – The remarkable true story of the epic horse trip made by the first people to travel Australia's then-unmarked Bicentennial National Trail. There are enough adventures here to satisfy even the most jaded reader.

Naysmith, Gordon, *The Will to Win* – This book recounts the only equestrian journey of its kind undertaken during the 20th century - a mounted trip stretching across 16 countries. Gordon Naysmith, a Scottish pentathlete and former military man, set out in 1970 to ride from the tip of the African continent to the 1972 Olympic Games in distant Germany.

Ondaatje, Christopher, *Leopard in the Afternoon* - The captivating story of a journey through some of Africa's most spectacular haunts. It is also touched with poignancy and regret for a vanishing wilderness – a world threatened with extinction.

Ondaatje, Christopher, *The Man-Eater of Pununai* – a fascinating story of a past rediscovered through a remarkable journey to one of the most exotic countries in the world — Sri Lanka. Full of drama and history, it not only relives the incredible story of a man-eating leopard that terrorized the tiny village of Punanai in the early part of the century, but also allows the author to come to terms with the ghost of his charismatic but tyrannical father.

Ondaatje, Christopher, *Sindh Revisited* – This is the extraordinarily sensitive account of the author's quest to uncover the secrets of the seven years Richard Burton spent in India in the army of the East India Company from 1842 to 1849. "If I wanted to fill the gap in my understanding of Richard Burton, I would have to do something that had never been done before: follow in his footsteps in India…" The journey covered thousands of miles—trekking across deserts where ancient tribes meet modern civilization in the valley of the mighty Indus River.

O'Connor, Derek, *The King's Stranger* – a superb biography of the forgotten Scottish explorer, John Duncan.

O'Reilly, Basha, *Count Pompeii – Stallion of the Steppes* – the story of Basha's journey from Russia with her stallion, Count Pompeii, told for children. This is the first book in the *Little Long Rider* series.

O'Reilly, CuChullaine, (Editor) *The Horse Travel Handbook* – this accumulated knowledge of a million miles in the saddle tells you everything you need to know about travelling with your horse!

O'Reilly, CuChullaine, (Editor) *The Horse Travel Journal* – a unique book to take on your ride and record your experiences. Includes the world's first equestrian travel "pictionary" to help you in foreign countries.

O'Reilly, CuChullaine, *Khyber Knights* – Told with grit and realism by one of the world's foremost

Other Titles

equestrian explorers, "Khyber Knights" has been penned the way lives are lived, not how books are written.

O'Reilly, CuChullaine, (Editor) *The Long Riders, Volume One* – The first of five unforgettable volumes of exhilarating travel tales.

Östrup, J, *(Swedish), Växlande Horisont* - The thrilling account of the author's journey to Central Asia from 1891 to 1893.

Patterson, George, *Gods and Guerrillas* – The true and gripping story of how the author went secretly into Tibet to film the Chinese invaders of his adopted country. Will make your heart pound with excitement!

Patterson, George, *Journey with Loshay: A Tibetan Odyssey* – This is an amazing book written by a truly remarkable man! Relying both on his companionship with God and on his own strength, he undertook a life few can have known, and a journey of emergency across the wildest parts of Tibet.

Patterson, George, *Patterson of Tibet* - Patterson was a Scottish medical missionary who went to Tibet shortly after the second World War. There he became Tibetan in all but name, adapting to the culture and learning the language fluently. This intense autobiography reveals how Patterson crossed swords with India's Prime Minister Nehru, helped with the rescue of the Dalai Lama and befriended a host of unique world figures ranging from Yehudi Menhuin to Eric Clapton. This is a vividly-written account of a life of high adventure and spiritual odyssey.

Pocock, Roger, *Following the Frontier* – Pocock was one of the nineteenth century's most influential equestrian travelers. Within the covers of this book is the detailed account of Pocock's horse ride along the infamous Outlaw Trail, a 3,000 mile solo journey that took the adventurer from Canada to Mexico City.

www.classictravelbooks.com

Pocock, Roger, *Horses* – Pocock set out to document the wisdom of the late 19th and early 20th Centuries into a book unique for its time. His concerns for attempting to preserve equestrian knowledge were based on cruel reality. More than 300,000 horses had been destroyed during the recent Boer War. Though Pocock enjoyed a reputation for dangerous living, his observations on horses were praised by the leading thinkers of his day.

Post, Charles Johnson, *Horse Packing* – Originally published in 1914, this book was an instant success, incorporating as it did the very essence of the science of packing horses and mules. It makes fascinating reading for students of the horse or history.

Ray, G. W., *Through Five Republics on Horseback* – In 1889 a British explorer - part-time missionary and full-time adventure junky – set out to find a lost tribe of sun-worshipping natives in the unexplored forests of Paraguay. The journey was so brutal that it defies belief.

Rink, Bjarke, *The Centaur Legacy* - This immensely entertaining and historically important book provides the first ever in-depth study into how man's partnership with his equine companion changed the course of history and accelerated human development.

Ross, Julian, *Travels in an Unknown Country* – A delightful book about modern horseback travel in an enchanting country, which once marked the eastern borders of the Roman Empire – Romania.

Ross, Martin and Somerville, E, *Beggars on Horseback* – The hilarious adventures of two aristocratic Irish cousins on an 1894 riding tour of Wales.

Ruxton, George, *Adventures in Mexico* – The story of a young British army officer who rode from Vera Cruz to Santa Fe, Mexico in 1847. At times the author exhibits a fearlessness which borders on insanity. He ignores dire warnings, rides through deadly deserts, and dares

Other Titles

murderers to attack him. It is a delightful and invigorating tale of a time and place now long gone.

von Salzman, Erich, *Im Sattel durch Zentralasien* – The astonishing tale of the author's journey through China, Turkistan and back to his home in Germany – 6000 kilometres in 176 days!

Schwarz, Hans *(German)*, *Vier Pferde, Ein Hund und Drei Soldaten* – In the early 1930s the author and his two companions rode through Liechtenstein, Austria, Romania, Albania, Yugoslavia, to Turkey, then rode back again!

Schwarz, Otto *(German), Reisen mit dem Pferd* – the Swiss Long Rider with more miles in the saddle than anyone else tells his wonderful story, and a long appendix tells the reader how to follow in his footsteps.

Scott, Robert, *Scott's Last Expedition* – Many people are unaware that Scott recruited Yakut ponies from Siberia for his doomed expedition to the South Pole in 1909. Here is the remarkable story of men and horses who all paid the ultimate sacrifice.

Shackleton, Ernest, *Aurora Australis* - The members of the British Antarctic Expedition of 1907-1908 wrote this delightful and surprisingly funny book. It was printed on the spot "at the sign of the Penguin"!

Skrede, Wilfred, *Across the Roof of the World* – This epic equestrian travel tale of a wartime journey across Russia, China, Turkestan and India is laced with unforgettable excitement.

The South Pole Ponies, *Theodore Mason* – The touching and totally forgotten story of the little horses who gave their all to both Scott and Shackleton in their attempts to reach the South Pole.

Stevens, Thomas, *Through Russia on a Mustang* – Mounted on his faithful horse, Texas, Stevens crossed the Steppes in search of adventure. Cantering across the pages of this classic tale is a cast of nineteenth century

www.classictravelbooks.com

Russian misfits, peasants, aristocrats—and even famed Cossack Long Rider Dmitri Peshkov.

Stevenson, Robert L., *Travels with a Donkey* – In 1878, the author set out to explore the remote Cevennes mountains of France. He travelled alone, unless you count his stubborn and manipulative pack-donkey, Modestine. This book is a true classic.

Strong, Anna Louise, *Road to the Grey Pamir* – With Stalin's encouragement, Strong rode into the seldom-seen Pamir mountains of faraway Tadjikistan. The political renegade turned equestrian explorer soon discovered more adventure than she had anticipated.

Sykes, Ella, *Through Persia on a Sidesaddle* – Ella Sykes rode side-saddle 2,000 miles across Persia, a country few European woman had ever visited. Mind you, she traveled in style, accompanied by her Swiss maid and 50 camels loaded with china, crystal, linens and fine wine.

Trinkler, Emile, *Through the Heart of Afghanistan* – In the early 1920s the author made a legendary trip across a country now recalled only in legends.

Tschiffely, Aimé, *Bohemia Junction* – "Forty years of adventurous living condensed into one book."

Tschiffely, Aimé, *Bridle Paths* – a final poetic look at a now-vanished Britain.

Tschiffely, Aimé, *Mancha y Gato Cuentan sus Aventuras* – The Spanish-language version of *The Tale of Two Horses* – the story of the author's famous journey as told by the horses.

Tschiffely, Aimé, *The Tale of Two Horses* – The story of Tschiffely's famous journey from Buenos Aires to Washington, DC, narrated by his two equine heroes, Mancha and Gato. Their unique point of view is guaranteed to delight children and adults alike.

Tschiffely, Aimé, *This Way Southward* – the most famous equestrian explorer of the twentieth century

Other Titles 79

decides to make a perilous journey across the U-boat infested Atlantic.

Tschiffely, Aimé, *Tschiffely's Ride* – The true story of the most famous equestrian journey of the twentieth century – 10,000 miles with two Criollo geldings from Argentina to Washington, DC. A new edition is coming soon with a Foreword by his literary heir!

Tschiffely, Aimé, *Tschiffely's Ritt* – The German-language translation of *Tschiffely's Ride* – the most famous equestrian journey of its day.

Ure, John, *Cucumber Sandwiches in the Andes* – No-one who wasn't mad as a hatter would try to take a horse across the Andes by one of the highest passes between Chile and the Argentine. That was what John Ure was told on his way to the British Embassy in Santiago-so he set out to find a few certifiable kindred spirits. Fans of equestrian travel and of Latin America will be enchanted by this delightful book.

Warner, Charles Dudley, *On Horseback in Virginia* – A prolific author, and a great friend of Mark Twain, Warner made witty and perceptive contributions to the world of nineteenth century American literature. This book about the author's equestrian adventures is full of fascinating descriptions of nineteenth century America.

Weale, Magdalene, *Through the Highlands of Shropshire* – It was 1933 and Magdalene Weale was faced with a dilemma: how to best explore her beloved English countryside? By horse, of course! This enchanting book invokes a gentle, softer world inhabited by gracious country lairds, wise farmers, and jolly inn keepers.

Weeks, Edwin Lord, *Artist Explorer* – A young American artist and superb writer travels through Persia to India in 1892.

Wentworth Day, J., *Wartime Ride* – In 1939 the author decided the time was right for an extended horseback ride through England! While parts of his country were being ravaged by war, Wentworth Day discovered an inland oasis of mellow harvest fields, moated Tudor farmhouses, peaceful country halls, and fishing villages.

Von Westarp, Eberhard, *Unter Halbmond und Sonne* – (German) – Im Sattel durch die asiatische Türkei und Persien.

Wilkins, Messanie, *Last of the Saddle Tramps* – Told she had little time left to live, the author decided to ride from her native Maine to the Pacific. Accompanied by her faithful horse, Tarzan, Wilkins suffered through any number of obstacles, including blistering deserts and freezing snow storms – and defied the doctors by living for another 20 years!.

Wilson, Andrew, *The Abode of Snow* – One of the best accounts of overland equestrian travel ever written about the wild lands that lie between Tibet and Afghanistan.

de Windt, Harry, *A Ride to India* – Part science, all adventure, this book takes the reader for a thrilling canter across the Persian Empire of the 1890s.

Winthrop, Theodore, *Saddle and Canoe* – This book paints a vibrant picture of 1850s life in the Pacific Northwest and covers the author's travels along the Straits of Juan De Fuca, on Vancouver Island, across the Naches Pass, and on to The Dalles, in Oregon Territory. This is truly an historic travel account.

Woolf, Leonard, *Stories of the East* – Three short stories which are of vital importance in understanding the author's mistrust of and dislike for colonialism, which provide disturbing commentaries about the disintegration of the colonial process.

Younghusband, George, *Eighteen Hundred Miles on a Burmese Pony* – One of the funniest and most enchanting books about equestrian travel of the nineteenth century, featuring "Joe" the naughty Burmese pony!

www.classictravelbooks.com

Other Titles

We are constantly adding new titles to our collections, so please check our websites:
        www.horsetravelbooks.com and
        www.classictravelbooks.com